intentionally blank

intentionally blank

Wilderness

no wilderness - no canaan

Rev Stella Adekunle

Jesus Joy Publishing

Published and printed in Great Britain in 2015 by
Jesus Joy Publishing, a division of Eklegein Ltd.

ISBN 978-1-90797-146-4

Jesus Joy Publishing
A division of Eklegein Ltd

www.jesusjoypublishing.co.uk
20151006

Dedication

This book is dedicated firstly to God - the Father, Son and Holy Spirit - who has never failed in backing up His calling upon my life.

To my wonderful husband, Isaac, who has been my rock and an encouragement to me in every way and in all matters of life. His love, care and support are highly cherished and can never be forgotten. Many thanks are extended to him for all he has done to support the work of God.

To both my spiritual and biological families for all their contributions. May God bless them all.

To the beloved men and women of God who are faithfully and relentlessly working to prepare the saints for the second coming of Christ and to all the saints in the world who are aspiring and waiting to see Jesus Christ at his return.

Rev Stella T Adekunle
Sword of the Spirit Evangelical Outreach
www.sseooutreach.org.uk

Acknowledgement

I would like to acknowledge my father in the Lord, Dr Daniel Olukoya (The General Overseer of Mountain of Fire and Miracle Ministries, World Wide). He is a father in need and in deed. He is truly a man of God. I pray that God will grant him more grace in Jesus' name.

Foreword

In order to get from your starting point in your Christian journey to the place that God has promised you, you must pass through the wilderness. For the children of Israel to move from the land of Egypt to the Promised Land of Canaan, they had to pass through the wilderness.

There is a necessary wilderness that we all need to pass through. Conversely, there is an unnecessary wilderness that many Christians pass through because of their disobedience to God.

The journey time across the wilderness for a small group of able bodied men was just eleven days. [Deuteronomy 1:2] However because it was an entire nation travelling with women, children and all their belongings, it took much longer. Hence, the Shekinah Glory Cloud [God's presence] that led them through the wilderness made them stop and camp at various intervals and for varied lengths of time. [Numbers 9:15-23]

Due to the size of the travelling group, the children of Israel could have passed through the Wilderness of Paran from

Goshen in Egypt to Kadesh Barnea in about nine months, but because of their continued rebellion, it took them forty long and troublesome years. And throughout this time, they were learning many important lessons.

Reverend Stella Adekunle has done a stellar job in unravelling the significance of the wilderness in the life of the Believer. She explains brilliantly how you can learn important lessons and discover the purposes of God during the dark days and dry parts of your spiritual journey. She explains the tests of faith you will encounter and how to overcome the hindrances the enemy brings along your path. Nonetheless she points out that there are blessings along this arduous journey as you make your way to the land of Canaan - the land that flows with divine milk and honey.

This book is about the realities of the Christian pilgrimage, it is about faith and giants, it is about challenges and victories, it is about walking with Jesus Christ in spite of hardships until we all as saints go marching in gloriously through the pearly gates of heaven!

What this anointed woman of God has written is essential reading for the serious Christian who wants to achieve all that God expects of them along life's narrow way. I trust you will be blessed as you read this book, not once, not twice, but several times.

In the harvest,

Dr Femi Olowo
Retired Principal, South London Christian College.
Principal, Global Christian Institute.
General Overseer, Jubilee International Churches.

Contents

Introduction

I give thanks to our Lord Jesus Christ who is the 'Author and Finisher of our faith' and the One who knows the end from the beginning. This book is written through the inspiration of God and it relates to the wilderness journey of the children of Israel to the promised land, what they faced in the wilderness and how God helped them through all their problems. It also illustrates the wilderness and Canaan experience of all children of God as we are rightly called the spiritual Israel. The hindrances or obstacles we encounter on the way to achieving the promises of God in our lives are the wilderness experiences of today. Therefore, as children of God, how can we handle the wilderness in our lives so that a forty-day journey will not become forty years as happened to the children of Israel?

As we journey through the wilderness, we need total reliance on our Lord Jesus Christ who also passed through His own 'wilderness experience' immediately after his baptism in the River Jordan. [This will also be discussed fully in this book] Whatever you are experiencing as your own wilderness, please cast all your burdens upon Jesus for He cares for you, and do not allow your short wilderness journey to become a journey of wandering. Learn to resist the devil and he will flee from you -

"Be sober, be vigilant; because your adversary the devil walks about like a roaring lion, seeking whom he may devour. Resist him, steadfast in the faith, knowing that the same sufferings are experienced by your brotherhood in the world."

[2 Peter 4:8-9]

Remember the Children of Israel kept on looking back to the lives they lived in Egypt and worshipped other gods in the wilderness. Because of this, they incurred the penalty for their disobedience from God -

"According to the number of the days in which you spied out the land, forty days, for each day you shall bear your guilt one year, namely forty years, and you shall know My rejection."

[Numbers 14:34]

This affected His promises for the generation that came out of Egypt.

May God in His mercy help us and give us the grace to abide in Him when going through our own wilderness experiences.

Most importantly, may God uphold us in the journey through this world which is the wilderness experience for every child of God, and guide us 'till we reach the promised land in Eternity -

> *"Then I, John, saw the holy city, New Jerusalem, coming down out of heaven from God, prepared as a bride adorned for her husband. And I heard a loud voice from heaven saying, 'Behold, the tabernacle of God is with men, and He will dwell with them, and they shall be His people. God Himself will be with them and be their God.'"*
>
> *[Revelation 21:2-3]*

Amen.

Chapter 1

Definition of Wilderness

The Meaning Of 'Physical Wilderness'

The wilderness is a desert, jungle and/or a place of waste according to the dictionary meaning.[1] Spiritually, a wilderness can be interpreted as field, which is a place of labour. According to Matthew - *"The field is the world"* [Matthew 13:38] Because of the nature of the terrain, no farmer would want to cultivate or farm in the wilderness no matter how hard-working he may be. There is nothing anyone can do to make the wilderness or desert fertile because this is how it is made by God who is the Creator of heaven and earth. Apart from being a place of waste, the wilderness is a place for wild animals to inhabit. It is a place of fear and terror.

Therefore, there must be a reason to go to the wilderness and those who goes will come out stronger because of the challenges which they have faced. For such a person wandering in the desert may result in hunger and thirst and in the loss of

---

1 The layman's Bible dictionary Edited by George W Knight and Rayburn W Ray.

strength and necessitate the loss one's possessions.

The Meaning Of 'Spiritual Wilderness'

From a spiritual perspective, the wilderness is a testing ground and sometimes a battleground, as well as a place of dryness and hunger for every believer. God sometimes uses the wilderness experience to check if we are doing His will:

> *"And you shall remember that the LORD your God led you all the way these forty years in the wilderness, to humble you and **test** you, to know what was in your heart, whether you would keep His commandments or not"*

> *[Deuteronomy 8:2]*

We will experience dryness in terms of a short period of want or lack of joy and hunger in terms of problems or difficulties. Going through the wilderness does not mean being outside of God's will, but it is a testing period to make us stronger and most importantly to establish our eternal right with Jesus Christ. A good example of this is the story of Lazarus and the rich man. [Luke 16:21-25] Many giants of faith went through this period and came back triumphant while many passed through and died in their wilderness. Jesus Christ also went through His own wilderness experience and He was not put to shame. Satan is the old devil and so whether you are young or even advanced in your Christian life, don't rely on your own knowledge, wisdom or strength to fight the wilderness battle but rely totally on the power that never fails - Jesus Christ. Remember He is the Lion of Judah and He has been tempted once in the wilderness by the devil after fasting and praying for forty days and nights. Therefore, there is nothing you are going through that He is not aware of. Cast your burdens unto Jesus because He cares for you:

"The poor and the needy seek water, but there is none, their tongue fail for thirst I, Lord, will hear them; I, the God of Israel, will not forsake them. I will open rivers in desolate heights, And fountains in the midst of the valleys; I will make the wilderness a pool of water, And the dry land springs of water."

[Isaiah 41:17-18]

Notes

1. There is always a purpose for the wilderness experience. [Deuteronomy 8:2, 7-9]

2. Sometimes desert or wilderness experiences come immediately after a 'Jordan River' experience, Jesus Christ being the prime example. So you too must also pass through Jordan in order to become a new creature in Christ. [2 Corinthians 5:17]

3. The wilderness experience is for spiritual maturity and self-assessment:

> *"Moreover Job continued his discourse, and said: 'As God lives, who has taken away my justice, and the Almighty, who has made my soul bitter, as long as my breath is in me, and the breath of God in my nostrils, my lips will not speak wickedness, nor my tongue utter deceit. Far be it from me that I should say you are right; till I die I will not put away my integrity from me...'"*
>
> *[Job 27:1-5]*

4. Even though it may seem as if you are alone in the wilderness, remember that God is there with you. God took care of the Israelites in the wilderness and He will take care of you. [Deuteronomy 29:5]

5. It is important to face the battle of the wilderness testing with *"the Sword of the Spirit which is the Word of God."* [Ephesians 6:17] When you have won the battle, don't let down your guard.

6. Learn to use the Word of God whether you are experiencing a physical or spiritual wilderness as Jesus did when Satan tempted Him - *"And they overcame him by the blood of the Lamb and by the word of their testimony..."* (Revelation 12:11)

Chapter 2

Burning Bush

God showed Moses this great vision before sending him to deliver the children of Israel from the land of slavery under the kingship of Pharaoh in Egypt:

> *"And the angel of the Lord appeared to him in a flame of fire from the midst of a bush. So he looked, and behold, the bush was burning with fire, but the bush was not consumed."*
>
> *[Exodus 3:2]*

God made His servant realise what the journey of the children of Israel from Egypt to Canaan would look like. God likened their journey to the burning bush that was not consumed. Everyone knows that fire is meant to destroy and consume things. The bush is meant to accelerate the burning, for as the oxygen helps in burning so also do the leaves and wood. It was in the midst of the bush that God told Moses that He had seen the oppression of His people in Egypt and heard their cry and had chosen Moses for their deliverance.

Why did God choose Moses? God saw in

Moses a man after His own heart who preferred to wear an imperishable crown rather than the perishable crown of the land of Egypt:

"By faith Moses, when he became of age, refused to be called the son of Pharaoh's daughter, choosing rather to suffer affliction with the people of God than to enjoy the passing pleasure of sin, esteeming the reproach of Christ greater riches than the treasures in Egypt; for he looked to the reward."
[Hebrews 11:24-26]

Moses refused at first to accept the offer but when God proved Himself as *"I am who I am"* [Exodus 3:14] and the One with the power to set His people free from a powerful ruler like Pharaoh, Moses accepted the task with faith.

God gave Moses instructions about the task ahead:

"Go and gather the elders of Israel together and say to them... 'I have surely visited you and seen what is done to you in Egypt and I have said I will bring you up out of the affliction of Egypt to the land of the Canaanites ... to a land flowing with milk and

honey.'"

[Exodus 3:16-17]

God gave the job description to Moses before sending him to Pharaoh. God showed Moses a great vision concerning the journey of the children of Israel from the land of slavery to the land flowing with milk and honey. The fire of the burning bush signifies what the children of Israel went through in Egypt. Pharaoh used them for hard labour yet they did not die; instead the Bible *indicates that:*

> *"... the more they afflicted them, the more they multiplied and grew. And they were in dread of the children of Israel. So the Egyptians made the children of Israel serve with rigor. And they made their lives bitter with hard bondage."*

[Exodus 1:12-14]

Fire also signifies the journey of the children of Israel through their wilderness experiences yet they reached Canaan as a nation. Do you know that the problems in your life are like fire burning the bush but not consuming it? Though it is rough and difficult, you will survive the problems and come out victorious. God declared:

> *"'And I will make you to this people a*

fortified bronze wall; and they will fight against you. But they shall not prevail against you; for I am with you to save you; and deliver you,' says the Lord."

[Jeremiah 15:20]

God proved Himself as the *"I am who I am"* to Moses in two other ways apart from revealing Himself through the burning bush which was not consumed.

He proved His supremacy through the rod in Moses' hand by turning it into a serpent and by turning Moses' hand leprous.

On both occasions God changed the situation back to normal as they were before. God used these signs to build up Moses' faith and trust in Him that He was able to move the unmovable and destroy the destroyer.

After all these experiences, Moses made himself available for God and this is why God used him. What about you, are you available for God to be used? Do you have faith and trust in the power that delivered the children of Israel from Egypt? If not, build up that faith now and give God the chance to come and deliver you from all your problems.

As Pharaoh's army was drowned in

the Red Sea, so also will God do to your enemies if you wait on Him. The *"I am who I am."* will also deal with the problems that have taken you captive and He will set you free by His power.

Before Moses went on the assignment, God reassured him about everything which caused doubt in his mind. Were it not for this, Moses would have doubted God when Pharaoh refused to let the children of Israel go:

> *"...You shall come, you and the elders of Israel, to the king of Egypt; and you shall say to him, The Lord God of the Hebrews has met with us, and now please, let us go three days journey into the wilderness, that we may sacrifice to the Lord our God. 'But I am sure that the king of Egypt will not let you go, no, not even by a mighty hand'"*

> *[Exodus 3:18-19]*

Truly God used His mighty hand to inflict different plagues on the Egyptians but Pharaoh hardened his heart until God brought death on the firstborn of each family who did not put the blood of the lamb on their door posts and lintels. Pharaoh's heart was hardened by God to wreaked vengeance on him concerning the children of Israel:

"Then I will harden Pharaoh's heart, so that he will pursue them, and I will gain honour over Pharaoh and over all his army, that the Egyptians may know that I am Lord..."

[Exodus 14:4 NKJV]

Eventually Pharaoh allowed the children of Israel to go after the death of all the Egyptians' firstborn:

"And it came to pass at midnight that the LORD struck all the firstborn in the land of Egypt, from the firstborn of Pharaoh who sat on his throne to the firstborn of the captive who was in the dungeon, and all the firstborn of livestock. So Pharaoh rose in the night, he, all his servants, and all the Egyptians; and there was a great cry in Egypt, for there was not a house where there was not one dead"

[Exodus 12:29-30]

Their journey through the wilderness to the Promised Land of Canaan took forty years.

Chapter 3

Achieving God's Purpose through the Wilderness Experience

It is certain that every believer will experience a testing period [wilderness] at least once in their lives. This will reveal to themselves the true state of their hearts:

"To everything there is a season, a time for every purpose under heaven"
[Ecclesiastes 3:1]

The wilderness experiences not only helps to assess your strengths and weaknesses and might eventually lead to promotion:

"And you shall remember that the Lord your God led you all the way these forty years in the wilderness, to humble you and test you, to know what was in your heart, whether you would keep His commandments or not."

[Deuteronomy 8:2]

The children of Israel went through the wilderness and God led them to the land of Canaan - the land that was filled with milk and honey. On the way they went through a lot of difficulties and experiences to test their faithfulness to God and to reveal that they were still mentally in Egypt despite God having freed them from their slavery.

Many times they disappointed God by grumbling asking why they were brought out of Egypt; clearly some preferred the slavery of their former lives. When the Israelites were hungry for food at the Wilderness of Sin they said:

> *"Oh, that we had died by the hand of the Lord in the land of Egypt, when we sat by the pots of meat and when we ate bread to the full! For you have brought us out into this wilderness to kill this whole assembly with hunger."*
>
> *[Genesis 16:3]*

The Israelites weakness and lack of spirit of long-suffering turned their wilderness experience to a wandering experience such that the journey that was supposed to last for a short time eventually took them forty years. It was God's intention for all to get to the land of Canaan, which was overflowing with milk and honey, but accepting the report of those ten spies changed the outcome for many:

> *"Because all these men who have seen*

*My glory and the signs which I did
in Egypt and in the wilderness, and
have put Me to the test now these ten
times, and have not heeded My voice,
they certainly shall not see the land of
which I swore to their fathers, nor shall
any of those who reject Me see it."*
[Numbers 14:22-23]

Notes

1. The Wilderness experience is to expose the weakness and strengths of the individual. The Israelites were tested and many times they disappointed God:

    *   At the Red Sea. [Exodus 14:10-13]

    *   At the Wilderness of Shur where there was no water to drink. [Exodus 15:22-26]

    *   At the Wilderness of Sin when they were hungry. [Exodus 16:3-6]

    *   At the camp at Rephidim where there was no water. [Exodus 17:1-6]

    *   They made a Golden calf. [Exodus 32:2-8]

    *   When the news about the inhabitants of Canaan were explained to the children of Israel

through the spies, they refused to enter the land but wanted a leader for themselves to take them back to Egypt. [Numbers 13:30-33, 14:1-4]

- The greatest disappointment was at Kadesh Barnea.

2. Each time the children of Israel disappointed God, He always proved Himself as One who never fails. Therefore, whatever your wilderness may be, don't grumble like the children of Israel. Remember God is able to back up His Word and He will never disappoint you, but it is important that you play your role and leave the rest to God.

3. The Wilderness experience leads to promotion only if endurance is used as a weapon to achieve success. Joseph went through a lot of problems during his own 'wilderness' experience:

- Being sold by his own blood brothers yet he was eventually victorious after many problems:

"Then Midianite traders passed by; so the brothers pulled Joseph up and lifted him to the Ishmalites for

twenty shekels of silver, and they took Joseph to Egypt."
[Genesis 37:28]

- He became a slave at Potiphar's house. [Genesis 39:1-2]

- He later ended up in the prison because he refused to sleep with his master's wife who wanted to commit the sin of adultery with him. [Genesis 39:7-9,20]

- But he persevered to the end and God promoted him to become the Prime Minister in a foreign land. Your wilderness is the path to glory.

"Then Pharaoh said to Joseph, 'In as much as God has shown you all this, there is no one as discerning and wise as you. You shall be over my house, and all my people shall be ruled according to your word; only in regard to the throne will I be greater than you'"
[Genesis 41:39-40]

4. The 'wilderness experience' is a temporary cross to bear, therefore try as much as possible to carry the cross and do not sin against God. Note that God is in the situation with you as He

promised through Isaiah:

"When you pass through the waters, I will be with you; and through the rivers, they shall not overflow you. When you walk through the fire, you shall not be burned, nor shall the flame scorch. For I am the Lord your God the Holy One of Israel your Saviour."

[Isaiah 43:2-3]

5. The three Hebrews [Shadrach, Meshach and Abed-Nego] were cast into the burning fiery furnace by king Nebuchadnezzar and God delivered them:

"Then king Nebuchadnezzar was astonished; and he rose in haste and spoke, saying to his counselors, 'Did we not cast three men bound into the midst of the fire?' They answered and said to the king, 'True, O king.' 'Look!' he answered, 'I see four men loose, walking in the midst of the fire; and they are not hurt, and the form of the fourth is like the Son of God.'"

[Daniel 3:24-26]

6. As Daniel was delivered from the den of lions, [Daniel 6:15-16] God will also deliver you from the lions troubling

your life. The 'lions' of your life are the problems that are aiming to swallow you up.

7. Job also went through a great loss. His wilderness was to test his faith in the Lord and in the end all his losses were restored double fold. The Bible states - *"Now the Lord blessed the latter days of Job more than his beginning..."* [Job 42:12]

8. Jabez grew up in poverty but God changed his life to prosperity. Likewise, God is able to change your situation. *"... so God granted him what he requested."* [1 Chronicles 4:10]

9. After many years of childlessness, God blessed Hannah with six children; therefore your situation is not impossible before God if you just trust in Him:

   "And the Lord visited Hannah, so that she conceived and bore three sons and two daughters."
   [1 Samuel 2:21]

10. There is purpose and seasons for everything under heaven. Though nobody knows the form and time of each individual's wilderness

experience, when it comes just note that it is for your promotion. The Bible warns:

"Because for every matter there is a time and judgement, though the misery of man increases greatly, for he does not know what will happen so who can tell him when it will occur?"

[Ecclesiastes 8:6-7]

11. The Wilderness is for the purpose of testing one's weaknesses and strength. So, whenever you are passing through your own wilderness, determine to identify your weaknesses and then try to work on them. The Israelites didn't deal with the 'spirit of Egypt' within them, and as a result they wandered in the wilderness for forty years instead of forty days:

"According to the numbers of the days in which you spied out the land, forty days, for each day you shall bear your guilt one year, namely forty years, and you shall know My rejection."

[Numbers 14:34]

Chapter 4

No Wilderness, No Canaan

God led the children of Israel through the wilderness rather than via the land of the Philistines so that when they saw war they would not return to Egypt. [Exodus 13:17-18]

The wilderness way would bring tests, and without tests there cannot be testimonies. Without battles there cannot be victory, and without examinations there cannot be certificates. Without problems there cannot be thanksgiving.

Before we arrive in our 'Promised Land' God needs us to know if we are capable of handling the position or blessings He is about to bestow.

It is essential that you also pass through your own wilderness before your Canaan. Even though you are chosen and elected of God, He will still use tested and tried vessels to contain His precious treasures.

Take note, Canaan, which stands for the promise of God in your life could be spiritual or material blessings, spiritual or physical promotion or movement from a lower to higher position.

We are tested and proven so that
we can be vessels of honour for the
Master's use:

> "Therefore if anyone cleanses himself
> ...he will be a vessel for honour,
> sanctified and useful for the Master,
> prepared for every good work."
> [2 Timothy 2:21]

Jesus was appointed and anointed before
His wilderness experience, yet He was
tempted by Satan to empower Him for
the tasks ahead of Him. The Wilderness
experience before arriving at Canaan,
is always geared to promote individual
endurance the key to success:

> "Indeed we count them blessed
> who endure. You have heard of the
> perseverance of Job and seen the end
> intended by the Lord-that the Lord is
> very compassionate and merciful"
> [James 5:11]

Here are some of the significant miracles
that God performed in the life of the
children of Israel during their wilderness
experience before they arrived at the
promised land:

1. A notable miracle happened at the
    Red Sea through Moses. It was there

that the east wind parted the Red Sea for the children of Israel to walk through on the 'dried land' and the same wind blew Pharaoh and his chariot into the Red Sea and killed them all:

"And Moses said to the people, do not be afraid. Stand still and see the salvation of the Lord which He will accomplish for you today, for the Egyptian whom you see today you shall see them no more forever."

[Exodus 14:13]

Truly God fought for the children of Israel. Most of the time, the path to your victory is the path to the destruction of your enemies. The Red Sea which served as a road to cross over for the children of Israel, also served as road to destruction for Pharaoh and the Egyptians' chariots.

2. God supplied water three times to the children of Israel in the wilderness:

- At Mount Horeb where God told Moses to strike the rock [Exodus 17:6] with his rod, and at Kadesh where He asked Moses to speak to the rock to release water [Numbers 20:8]

- At the Wilderness of Zin, there
  was no water for the children of
  Israel. This was where the people
  unknowingly provoked Moses to
  sin against God. He struck the rock
  instead of speaking as God had
  directed and thereby he sinned
  against God. [Numbers 20:7-12]

- At the Wilderness of Shur, God
  turned the bitterness of Marah
  waters to sweet through Moses:

*"... he cried out to the LORD, and
the LORD showed him a tree. When
he cast it into the waters, the
waters were made sweet. There He
made a statute and an ordinance
for them, and there He tested
them"*

[Exodus 15:25 KJV]

- If God used the above methods to
  change situations for the children
  of Israel, He can do the same for
  you. There is absolutely nothing God
  cannot do to save or change the
  situation of anyone who trusts in
  Him. Remember the Prophet Elisha,
  He used a stick to cause an iron
  axe that fell into the water to float.
  [2 Kings 6:6] God always delights
  in using the weak to defeat the

strong; therefore, don't give up hope. Jesus Christ is at your door to bless you and remove your own problems just as he has done for others in the past, so why not give Him the opportunity?

3. God rained down bread from Heaven everyday of the wilderness journey. The Lord said to Moses -

"Behold, I will rain bread from heaven for you, and the people shall go out and gather a certain quota every day, that I may test them, whether they will walk in My law or not."

[Exodus 16:4]

For forty years in the wilderness, God fed the Israelites with heavenly manna and they never went hungry. Therefore, if you also eat heavenly food which is the Word of God, you will never be hungry again.

God also fed the Prophet Elijah in the wilderness when Jezebel, the wife of king Ahab, threatened to kill him.

Trust in God and He will provide manna for you during your own wilderness experience. He is the One who can supply all your needs; so whatever you lack, tell God because He is ready to hear and answer you:

"For the Lord will comfort Zion, He will comfort all Her waste places; He will make her wilderness like Eden, and her desert like the garden of the Lord; joy and gladness will be found in it..."

[Isaiah 51:3]

This is a comfort to those currently experiencing their own time of testing.

4. God gave the Israelites victory over the Amalikites. While they were in the Wilderness at Rephidim, the Israelites came across the Amalekites who fought with them and yet the children of Israel prevailed. They prevailed because:

- They co-operated in the battle.

"Moses said to Joshua, 'Choose us some men and go out, fight with Amalek. Tomorrow I will stand on the top of the hill with the rod of God in my hand.'"

[Exodus 17:9]

The children of God won the

battle before it started because of unity among them. None of them considered himself more important than Moses. They all obeyed him as God had directed and they eventually won the battle. Sometimes you need other people to fight the battle of your life. Most importantly, be sure that the people involved are children of God.

- God's purpose for the children of Israel had to be fulfilled and God fought against every hindrance that wanted to frustrate the fulfilment of God's purpose for their journey. His purpose for the children of Israel was to set them free from the Egyptian's slavery and not to kill them. *"If God is for us, who can be against us?"* [Romans 8:31] The purpose of God for your life is to set you free from all your problems whether physical or spiritual and not to die [second death Revelation 20:14], for it is written - *"Therefore if the Son makes you free, you shall be free indeed."* [John 8:36]

God is ready to fight for you if you commit the battles of your life to Him instead of fighting for yourself.

Cast your burdens on Him because He cares for you and He will fight for you. *"The Lord will fight for you and you shall hold your peace"* [Exodus 14:14]

- They won the battle because they knew the strategies necessary for victory. Moses spread out the armies of the Lord to advantageous areas according to God's direction:

"So Joshua did as Moses said to him, and fought with Amalek, and Moses, Aaron, and Hur went up to the top of the hill."
[Exodus 17:10]

As Moses did, you must learn to 'spread out' your spiritual weapons in order to hit the target and come out victoriously. 'Spread out' in terms of your prayer points and don't limit the power of God in your prayers. It is important to follow God's direction at all times as this is what can give you victory. Sometimes it is necessary to include fasting as well as praying and meditating on the Word of God. Notably, Moses also lifted up the 'rod of God' [Word] in his hand for victory through the wilderness experiences.

Chapter 5

The Ever-Vigilant Eye

God kept the children of Israel through their journey in the wilderness. He never allowed any evil to befall them. The psalmist reminds us:

> "..He who keeps you will not slumber. Behold He who keeps Israel shall neither slumber nor sleep. The Lord is your keeper; the Lord is your shade at your right hand. The sun shall not strike you by day, nor the moon by night. The Lord shall preserve you from all evil"
>
> [Psalms 121:3-7]

Even though many times they showed themselves to be ingrates through their disobedience to God, He still stood by His promise to them:

> "And the Lord said: I have surely seen the oppression of My people who are in Egypt, and have heard their cry because of their taskmasters, for I know their sorrows. So I have come down to deliver them..."
>
> [Exodus 3:7-8]

God's eyes watched over the children
of Israel throughout their journey. He
started with the Passover. He asked the
children of Israel to mark their doorposts
with the blood of the lambs and when the
LORD [Yahweh] passed through the land:

*"For the LORD will pass through to
strike the Egyptians; and when He
sees the blood on the lintel and on the
two doorposts, the Lord will pass over
the door and not allow the destroyer to
come into your houses to strike you."*
[Exodus 12:23]

God appointed the pillar of cloud in the day
and pillar of fire in the night to guide them:

*"And the Lord went before them by day
in a pillar of cloud to lead the way, and
by night in a pillar of fire to give them
light, so as to go by day and night. He
did not take away the pillar of cloud by
day or pillar of fire by night."*
[Exodus 13:21]

He gave this for directions and miracles
throughout the journey but also gave
them the law. It was in the wilderness
God gave the children of Israel the ten
commandments and many other rules
and regulations were given to them to
prevent them from going astray in

the wilderness. Many times the Israelites mourned and grumbled in the wilderness for food, water and many other things but God, who sees and knows our needs, always answered them and proved that 'He who watches over Israel never sleeps nor slumbers'.

Have you recognised your own wilderness?

What is your problem?

Are they spiritual or material problems?

I want you to know that God is watching over you. Even when it seems that you are alone or forgotten in your problem, God is with you and His angels are standing by. Before Jesus' started His ministry, He went into the wilderness where He was tempted by Satan. If it happened to Jesus and He prevailed, be assured that if you trust Him you will also prevail. With Christ on your side you are more than a conqueror. Mark records:

"... Jesus was there in the wilderness forty days, tempted by Satan, and was with the wild beasts; and the angels ministered to Him."

[Mark 1:13]

Lessons

1. *"Cast your burden on the Lord. And He shall sustain you He shall never permit the righteous to be moved."* [Psalms 55:22] No matter what your problem is, just come to God. He loves the believers so much they are called the 'apple of His eye':

   > *"For thus says the Lord of hosts: 'He sent me after glory, to the nations which plunder you; for he who touches you touches the apple of His eye.'"*
   >
   > *[Zechariah 2:8 KJV]*

   As you would be careful about allowing anything to touch your eye, so also God will protect you. Even though you feel alone in your problem, He is watching over you.

2. Allow God's staff and rod to comfort you [Psalm 23] during your time in the wilderness.

   Remember the rod of God in Moses' hand performed many miracles and it was the source of comfort in time of need for the children of Israel.

   The rod of God to you today is the power of His Word in the Bible and the Holy Spirit - the greatest Comforter. Let them continually strengthen you and comfort you in your problems. Have in mind always that it may be tough, yet you will not die in your problems but you shall be an overcomer. Amen.

3. Wait on the Lord in prayers for instruction and direction. Whoever endures to the end shall be saved:

> *"But those who wait on the Lord shall renew their strength; they shall mount up with wings like eagles, they shall run and not be weary, they shall walk and not faint."*
>
> *[Isaiah 40:31]*

Chapter 6

Wilderness Experiences

The Wilderness Experience Of Hunger

The Israelites reached a point of hunger
early in the journey and complained bitterly
against God. They accused Moses and
Aaron for bringing them out of Egypt to die:

> *"And the children of Israel said to
> them, 'Oh, that we had died by the
> hand of the Lord in the land of Egypt,
> when we sat by the pots of meat and
> when we ate bread to the full! For
> you have brought us out into this
> wilderness to kill this whole assembly
> with hunger.'"*
>
> *[Exodus 16:3]*

The Israelites offended through their lack of
verbal self control. If it was God's intention
to kill them, He would not have sent Moses
to the land of Egypt to free them, and He
would not have subjected Moses to all the
trouble of convincing Pharaoh through signs
and wonders that God was speaking to him.

If care is not taken when you are passing
through the wilderness experience, your
perception of what God is doing may lead

you to become aggressive and this was exactly what happened to the Israelites. Remember God is your sufficiency and He is able to deliver you at all times; He who used His iron hand to bring the Israelites out of Egypt was more than capable of providing for their needs but He made them wander in the wilderness to test them. He said:

> *"... remember that the Lord your God led you all the way these forty years in the wilderness, to humble you and test you, to know what was in your heart, whether you would keep His commandments or not."*
>
> *[Deuteronomy 8:2]*

Your 'wilderness' is a time of testing so you can better understand your relationship with God. Endurance, perseverance, prayerfulness and meditating on the Word of God is the key to your success.

Lessons

1. The Wilderness of hunger is only for a period. Endurance and perseverance are the weapons for success:

   > *"The end of a thing is better than its beginning, the patient in spirit is*

better than the proud in spirit."
[Ecclesiastes 7:8]

2. Fear of God will always sustain you in the wilderness of hunger. Joseph feared God and resisted Potiphar's wife's attempt to seduce him so God promoted him. We are told that:

    "... he refused and said to his master's wife, 'Look, my master does not know what is with me in the house, and he has committed all that he has to my hand. There is no one greater in this house than I, nor has he kept back anything from me but you, because you are his wife. How then can I do this great wickedness, and sin against God?'"
    [Genesis 39:8-9]

3. The wilderness experience may manifest as a lack of joy, poverty, illness, diseases, war, desolation, famine, betrayal or desertion from friends and family. Do not let your love for Christ grow cold because of all these. The Apostle Paul challenges us to consider:

    "Who shall separate us from the love of Christ? Shall tribulation, or distress, or persecution, or famine,

or nakedness, or peril, or sword?"
[Romans 8:35]

Each element in the above list is capable of separating believers from the love of Christ; therefore, watch out!

4. Do not rely on any other gods no matter what you are going through in the wilderness experience. The Israelites worshipped other gods in the wilderness and therefore provoked God's wrath, wasted their valuable time, and most of them died in the wilderness.

   Though they did get to Canaan as a nation, it took longer than it might have if they had been obedient. [Jeremiah 25:6]

   Other 'gods' may be your wealth, position, possessions, friends, family, work, children, husband or wife. Do not place them above the will of God in your life as this could lead to missing His promises for you as did the Israelites.

5. Totally rely on God for your manna - heavenly food. Physically God is able to supply all your needs. [Matthew 6:25-

34] Spiritually, He is the 'bread of life' for you through the Word of God from which you will eat and never hunger again:

" And Jesus said to them – 'I am the bread of life. He who comes to Me shall never hunger and he who believes in Me shall never thirst.'"

[John 6:35]

6. Jesus confirmed that doing the will of God was His own food *"... my food is to do the will of the one who sent Me, and to finish His work."* [John 4:34] Likewise it is also important for you to keep doing the will of God as your daily food.

7. The wilderness may come in the form of poverty or debt and Satan might want to use this to push you to the edge by sending people to lure you into temptation.

   He may even send the spirit of covetousness to you to tempt you to steal or join a 'bad gang' to survive.

   Never allow Satan to trick you into sinning against God. Jesus had the same experience after His praying and fasting for forty days and nights.

Satan tempted Him with food:

"Now when the tempter came to Him, he said, 'If You are the Son of God, command these stones become to bread.' But He answered and said, 'it is written, Man shall not live by bread alone, but by every word that proceeds from the mouth of God.'"

[Matthew 4:3-4]

If Satan could test Jesus Christ, then he will test you as followers of Christ to see whether you will bow down to him or not.

8. Hunger can easily make you give in to temptation. The Bible records that a prophet of God died because he disobeyed God. God sent him on an errand to confront and warn Jeroboam who was engaging in idolatry; God instructed the prophet not to drink or eat throughout his journey; but an old prophet tricked him into eating. He went back with the old prophet, ate and died of disobedience:

"Thus says the Lord: 'because you have disobeyed the word of the Lord, and have not kept the commandment... but you came

*back, ate bread and drank water
in the place of which the Lord said
to you, Eat no bread and drink no
water, your corpse shall not come
to the tomb of your fathers.'"*

[1 Kings 13:21-22]

Be careful not to disobey God in the wilderness of testing as this could lead to both spiritual and physical death. Trust in the Lord for whatever you lack and He will provide for all your needs. He is Jehovah Jireh, the God who provides for us.

The Wilderness Experience Of Thirst

On three occasions, the children of Israel experienced thirst in the wilderness and on each occasion, God did not disappoint them:

1. At the Wilderness of Shur when they went for three days in the wilderness without water. But when they got to Marah they could not drink the water there for it was bitter. [Marah means 'bitter'] God instructed Moses to cast a tree into the waters when then became sweet to drink.

2. At Horeb where God commanded Moses:

   "Behold, I will stand before you

there on the rock in Horeb; and you
shall strike the rock, and water will
come out of it, that the people may
drink.' and Moses did so..."

[Exodus 17:6]

3. At Kadesh where there was no water
    for the congregation of Israel. Moses
    prayed to God and He responded by
    instructing Moses to speak to the
    rock before the Israelites and it would
    bring forth water:

    "Take the rod; you and your
    brother Aaron gather the
    congregation together. Speak to
    the rock before their eyes, and it
    will yield its water; thus you shall
    bring water."

[Numbers 20:8]

But Moses did contrary to God's
commandment, and sinned because
of the pressure from the congregation
of Israel:

"And Moses and Aaron gathered the
congregation together before the
rock and he said to them: hear now
you rebels! must we bring water for
you out of this rock? Then Moses
lifted his hand and struck the rock
twice with his rod; and water and

*the water came out abundantly,
and the congregation and their
animals drank, Then the Lord spoke
to Moses and Aaron, because you
did not believe me... therefore you
shall not bring this congregation
into the land which I have given
them."*

[Numbers 20:10-12]

Even with all that Moses had done, this sin kept him from entering the Promised Land.

- What is your own wilderness experience of thirst?

- What do you thirst for or what do you want desperately to quench your dryness?

No matter what it is, surrender to God. He has the power to quench your thirst since He did the same for the children of Israel. He will not deny you the desire of your heart since *"Jesus is same yesterday, today and for ever."* [Hebrews 13:8] Just as He supplied water in the wilderness, He will also supply water in the desert of your life. [Isaiah 48:21]

Lessons

1. Be careful not to allow the pressure of people around you or your heart's desire to cause you to rebel against God as Moses did.

2. Jesus is the water of life; tap into the living water today and you shall never thirst again. Jesus gives the assurance that:

   "... whoever drinks of the water that I shall give him will never thirst but the water that I shall give him will become in him fountain of water springing up into everlasting life."
   [John 4:14]

3. Just as God changed the Marah waters from bitter to sweet, whatever is bitter in your personal life, family or business will change to sweet; but you must believe in the power that can change the unchangeable. Note that there is no impossibility in the dictionary of God - *"For with God nothing will be impossible."* [Luke 1:27]

4. At Marah, God asked Moses to cast the tree into the river to change the water from bitter to sweet; therefore, God can use anything to change the

situation of your life. Learn not to argue or question God when He gives you an instruction. We must always trust God because - *"the foolishness of God is wiser than men, and the weakness of God is stronger than men."* [1 Corinthians 1:25,27]

The Wilderness Experience Of War

The children of Israel fought a lot of wars during their journey from Egypt to Canaan. All along God proved Himself as a Mightier warrior - *"The Lord is a man of war. The Lord is His name."* [Exodus 15:3] There were two major wars they won on their journey:

War Against The Amalekites

The Amalekites were descendents of Esau, Amalek was son of Eliphaz and Timna, the concubine. Therefore, the Amalekites originated from the son born through fornication:

> *"Now Timna was the concubine of Eliphaz, Esau's son, and she bore Amalek to Eliphaz..."*
>
> *[Genesis 36:12]*

Since God loves humanity but hates sin, He will not allow His Own elect to be tampered with.

The Amalekites came to fight the children of Israel at Rephidim, but God defeated them by His rod in Moses hand. When the rod of God in Moses' hand was lifted up, the Israelites had the upper hand, and when it was lowered the Amalekites had the upper hand. But by working together and letting Moses sit while Aaron and Hur supported his hands, Moses' hands were steady. With Moses' hand lifted up and Joshua at the battle front, God defeated the Amalekites.

The Battle At Jericho

Immediately the children of Israel crossed Jordan they faced the battle at Jericho. When they arrived at Jericho, it was securely shut up because of the children of Israel. [Joshua 6:1] God promises:

> *"I will go before you and make the crooked places straight; I will break in pieces the gates of bronze And cut the bars of iron. I will give you the treasures of darkness And riches of secret places..."*
>
> *[Isaiah 45:2-3]*

This is exactly what God did for the children of Israel - He went before them to demolish the wall of Jericho even before the Israelites won the battle. God commanded the children of Israel through Joshua:

> "... 'see! I have given Jericho into your hand, its king, and the mighty men of Valour. You shall march around the city, all you men of war; you shall go all around the city once. This you shall do six days... But the seventh day you shall march again around the city seven times, and the priests shall blow the trumpets... all the people shall shout with a great shout; then the wall of the city will fall down flat.'"

> [Joshua 6:2-5]

Lessons

1. Moses lifted up the rod of God in his hand for victory. Do likewise by lifting up your hands to God through your prayers and thanks. We have the assurance that *"The eyes of the Lord are on the righteous, and His ears are open to their cry."* [Psalms 34:15]

2. The obedience of the children of Israel gave them victory at Jericho. Learn not to argue with God on any instructions given to you. Be humble for God to elevate you:

> *"No good thing will He withhold from those who walk uprightly. O*

Lord of hosts blessed is the man
who trusts in You!"
[Psalm 84:11-12]

3. The shout of the children of Israel caused the wall of Jericho to fall; likewise, God can use anything to bring victory to you. If God can use a donkey to speak to Balaam [Numbers 22:20-30], and ravens to bring food for Elijah [1 King 17:6], then He can use anything to sort out your wilderness problems:

    "Behold, I am the Lord the God of all flesh. Is there anything too hard for Me?"
    [Jeremiah 32:27]

4. Do not stand in the way of anyone's progress because as God cursed and defeated Amalek. [Exodus 17:13-16] He could do the same to you. God jealously guards the lives of His believers so He will not allow anything to hinder or touch His elect - *"... And He shall never permit the righteous to be moved."* [Psalm 55:22]

5. The Bible recorded that the Amalekites and the people of Jericho were defeated by the edge of the sword. [Exodus 17:13, Joshua 6:21]

Today, our sword of the spirit is the Word of God, and our main battlefield is the heart because the heart is deceitful and it is the heart that Satan always targets. Therefore - *"take the helmet of salvation, and the sword of the spirit which is the Word of God"* [Ephesians 6:17] to fight the battle.

Chapter 7

The Wilderness Experience as a Test of Faith

God led the children of Israel through the wilderness to test their hearts to see whether or not they would forsake Him, but they failed the test on many occasions. He declared to them:

> *"And you shall remember that the Lord your God led you all the way this forty years in the wilderness, to humble you and **test you to know what was in your heart,** whether you will keep His commandments or not."*
>
> *[Deuteronomy 8:2]*

From this, we know that God tested the children of Israel in the wilderness. Two of the many tests of faith were:

- Crossing the Red Sea.
- Crossing River Jordan.

Crossing The Red Sea

God's strong hand brought the children of Israel out of Egypt. Their first wilderness experience was at the Red Sea where

Pharaoh was pursuing them in chariots and there only the Red Sea in front of them. The children of Israel reached the point whereby they couldn't go forward or backward so they naturally thought that the end had come. This doubt was revealed in their statement to Moses:

"Is this not the word that we told you in Egypt, saying 'let us alone that we may serve the Egyptians?'...than that we should die in the wilderness"

[Exodus 14:12]

Moses demonstrated his great faith here by his words of encouragement. Instead of panicking, Moses stood as a solider of God and told the children of Israel:

"Do not be afraid. Stand still and see the salvation of the Lord... for the Egyptians whom you see today, you shall see again no more. The Lord will fight for you and you shall hold your peace."

[Exodus 14:13-15]

God instructed Moses to stretch out his hand over the sea. He did so and the Lord caused the sea to roll back by a strong east wind all that night. The next day the children of Israel to crossed over on the dry land. Then God instructed Moses:

*"Stretch out your hand over the sea,
that the waters may come back upon
the Egyptians, on their chariots, and
on their horsemen."*

[Exodus 14:26]

Truly God fought for the children of Israel because the same waters that favoured them, destroyed and killed Pharaoh and his soldiers. They relied on God by taking the step of faith to walk through the parted Red Sea without questioning Him. What about you? Would you not have queried or argued with Moses?

Crossing the River Jordan

Another place where we see the children of Israel exercise faith was at the River Jordan under the leadership of Joshua. Just as God commanded Moses at the Red Sea to stretch his hand over the sea, He commanded Joshua that as soon as the feet of the priest who bore the ark of the Lord rested in the waters of Jordan, the water would be cut off. This paved the way for another miraculous crossing for the children of Israel:

*"Then the priest who brought the ark
of the covenant of the Lord stood
firm on dry ground in the midst of the
Jordan; and all Israel crossed over on*

the dry ground until all the people had
crossed completely over the Jordan."

[Joshua 3:15-17]

Lessons

1. Have faith in the Lord and He will
   never disappoint you. Believe in the
   name of Jesus Christ and it shall be
   well with you. Jesus promises that:

   "...if you have faith as a mustard
   seed, you will say to this mountain,
   'Move from here to there,' and
   it will move; and nothing will be
   impossible for you."

   [Matthew 17:20]

2. Just as the children of Israel were
   able to cross over the Red Sea, God
   will part every 'Red Sea' in your
   life if you believe in the Power who
   helped the children Israel. As Moses
   declared:

   "Do not be afraid. Stand still, and
   see the salvation of the Lord which
   He will accomplish for you today.
   For the Egyptians [problems] *who*
   you see today, you shall see again
   no more forever."

   [Exodus 14:13]

3. On both occasions, the children of

Israel walked on dry land because they trusted in the Power who can do the impossible. Though it may seem tough and rough, don't give up and be of good courage for our Lord Jesus Christ has conquered the world. Therefore trust totally in God and He will not fail you - "*... above all, take the shield of faith with which you will quench all the fiery darts of the wicked one.*" [Ephesians 6:16]

4. *"For we walk by faith, not by sight"* [2 Corinthians 5:7] Learn to walk by faith and not by what you see. Though by human reasoning, it seemed to be the end for the children of Israel, they walked by faith and not by the overwhelming evidence of what was in front of them – the Red Sea, and behind them - Pharaoh and his chariots. Without questioning how Moses would enable them to cross the Red Sea, they believed what he said and took the step of faith. Don't place the problems of your life above the power of God. As Jesus declared - "*... With men this is impossible, but with God all things are possible.*" [Matthew 19:26]

Chapter 8

Hindrances to Reaching Canaan

Hindrances are what stand in the way of the fulfilment of the promises of God for our lives. These are the delays we can experience along the way. The children of Israel encountered many hindrances in the wilderness that delayed the promise of the Lord in their lives. Some were caused by the distractions from their enemies while most were caused by themselves. Part of the distractions came from those kings who would not allow them to pass through or cross their territories. The book of Joshua records:

> "... when all the kings of Amorites who were on the west side of Jordan, and all kings of the Canaanites who were by the sea, heard the Lord had dried up the waters of the Jordan from before the children of Israel until we had crossed over, that their heart melted; and there was no spirit in them any longer because of the children of Israel"
>
> [Joshua 5:1]

While some of the delays were cause by

nature, they supernaturally reached the Red Sea [Exodus 14:13-16] and the River Jordan. [Joshua 3:16-17]

Most importantly, the major delay that caused them to journey for forty years came from the children of Israel. God declared:

> *"According to the number of the days in which you spied out the land forty days, for each day you shall bear your guilt one year, namely forty years, and you shall know My rejection..."*
> [Numbers 14:34-35]

Remember those encouraging words from scripture - *"If God is for us who can be against us?"* [Romans 8:31] This is a rhetorical question to which you need to supply your own answer. Truly God was for the children of Israel but they blocked his blessings. Throughout their journey, whenever they were facing problems, they always looked back to what they left behind in Egypt by complaining to Moses:

> *"Is this not the word that we told you in Egypt saying, 'let us alone that we may serve the Egyptians?' For it would have been better for us to serve the Egyptians than that we should die in*

the wilderness.'"

[Exodus 14:12, 16:3, 17:3]

To make matters worse, they kept forgetting the commandment of the Lord - *"You shall have no other gods before me. You shall not make yourself a carved image ..."* [Exodus 20:3-4] Two examples of this are:

Firstly, when Moses was delayed on the mountain, the people confronted Aaron and said to him:

> *"'come make us gods that shall go before us'... and Aaron said to them break off the golden earring which are in the ears of your wives, your sons and your daughters and bring them to me... and he fashioned it an engraving tool, and make a moulded calf. Then said, 'this is your god O Israel...'"*
>
> *[Exodus 32:2-4]*

Secondly, they worshipped Baal of Peor - *"For Israel joined to Baal of Peor and the anger of the Lord was aroused against Israel."* [Numbers 25:3]

On each occasion, God's anger was aroused against them and this made Him punish them. But what made God change the duration of their journey was when they planned to choose a replacement to Moses who would lead them back to Egypt after hearing the reports about Canaan from the spies:

> "Why has the Lord brought us to this land to fall by the sword, that our wives and children should become victim? Will it not be better for us to return to Egypt? So they said to one another, 'Let us select a leader and return to Egypt'"
>
> [Numbers 14:3-4]

Because our God is a convenant-keeping God, He is not a man [human] who lies and whatever He says, He does. The children of Israel disobeyed God, yet the promise of God for them concerning Canaan remained. God cared for them even though they were not faithful. God punished the adult generation that came out of Egypt but fulfilled His promise for the benefit of the descendants after them. He declared:

> "Because all this men who have seen my glory and the signs which I did in Egypt and in the Wilderness, and have put Me to the test now these ten times and have not heeded My voice, they shall certainly not see the land which I swore to their fathers, nor shall any of those who rejected Me see it. But My servant Caleb, because he has a

different spirit in him and has followed
Me fully, I will bring into the land
where he went, and his descendants
shall inherit."

[Numbers 14:23-24]

God fulfilled this under Joshua's leadership.
[Joshua 5:6-7]

Lessons

1. Be aware of things that could hinder
    the promises of God for your life. The
    Bible encourages us to *"watch and
    pray"*. Learn to disassociate yourself
    from the so-called friends who could
    cause distractions.

2. Be aware of your priorities so that
    you will not be easily distracted. The
    children of Israel were distracted by
    their immediate needs and lusted
    after vain things. Also, Moses was
    delayed from coming down from
    the Mountain which changed their
    focus. Their notable impatience and
    intolerance caused them to undermine
    the will of God for their lives. He
    declared:

    *"I have led you forty years in the
    wilderness. Your clothes have not
    worn out on you, and your sandals*

have not worn out on your feet."
[Deuteronomy 29:5]

Yet, the children of Israel still went after other gods. They were not satisfied with the signs and wonders performed by God so they moulded a golden calf for themselves.

3. The children of Israel served other gods and God punished them. Though the Israelites reached the land of Canaan, the generation that came out of Egypt did not:

    "For the children of Israel walked forty years in the wilderness, till all the people who were men of war, [over the age of 20] *who came out of Egypt, were consumed, because they did not obey the voice of the Lord ... to whom the Lord swore that He would not show them the land which the Lord had sworn to their fathers that He would give us, a land flowing with milk and honey."*
    [Joshua 5:6]

    Take care so that what God has for you, shall not be postponed or re-directed to benefit the generation after you.

4. Although Romans reminds us that *"if God is for us, who can be against us?"* [Romans 8:31], we can act against our own interests. Because the children of Israel acted against their own best interests, many did not get to the Promised Land.

5. God commanded the children of Israel as follows - *"For you shall not serve other gods, for the Lord, whose name is Jealous is a jealous God."* [Exodus 34:14] However, the children of Israel went against this and served other gods thereby continuously displeasing God and so missing the blessings He had planned.

    In what ways are you also serving other gods?

    It is true you may not have a shrine or golden image of a calf but what about those things you have given greater priority to than God, or that you adore and worship in the corner of the room where no one can see?

    Don't forget that God's eyes are everywhere:

    "'Can anyone hide himself in secret places, so I shall not see him?' says

the LORD; 'Do I not fill heaven and earth?' says the LORD."

[Jeremiah 23:23-24]

People may not be able to see it written on your face that you serve other gods but God sees it:

"... For the Lord does not see as man sees; for man looks at the outward appearance, but the Lord looks at the heart."

[1 Samuel 16:7]

6. Caleb and his descendants received the blessing of God because a different spirit was found in him from the spirit in the rest of the children of Israel besides Joshua. God promised:

"...My servant Caleb, because he has a different spirit in him and has followed Me fully, I will bring into the land ... and his descendants shall inherit it."

[Numbers 14:22-24]

Do you know that God can change your family situation just because of you? Be filled with the Holy Spirit at all times and serve our Lord Jesus Christ in truth and in spirit.

Chapter 9

The Wilderness Experience of Blessing

The wilderness was not only a place of war, hunger and thirst for the children of Israel but a place of blessing. God even blessed them before they left Egypt. He told Moses:

> *"And I will give this people favour in the sight of the Egyptians; and it shall be, when you go, that you shall not go empty-handed. But every woman shall ask of her neighbour, namely, of her who dwells near her house, articles of silver, articles of gold, and clothing... So you shall plunder the Egyptians."*
> *[Exodus 4:21-22]*

Also through the vengeance of God on the Midianites, He blessed the children of Israel. God took vengeance on the Midianites because they harassed the children of Israel with their schemes *and caused them to commit harlotry with the women of Moab and sacrificed to their gods called Baals of Peor. [Number 25:1-18]*

> *"They warred against Midianites, just as the Lord commanded Moses, and*

*they killed all the males...and the
children of Israel took the women of
Midian captive with their little ones and
took as spoil all their cattle, all their
flocks and all their goods."*

[Numbers 31:7-9]

At the battle at Jericho, God also blessed
the children of Israel:

*"And you, by all means abstain from
the accursed things lest you become
accursed when you take of the
accursed things and make the camp of
Israel a curse, and trouble it. But all
the silver and the gold, and vessels of
gold and iron, are consecrated to the
Lord; they shall come to the treasury
of the Lord."*

[Joshua 6:18-19, 24]

And the children of Israel obeyed God's
commandment. Our God is a convenant-
keeping God. Whatever He says He will
do, nothing can stop Him. God promised
Abraham and his descendants that He
would give them Canaan as a possession
and bless them and so He did. He promised
that:

*"Blessing I will bless and multiplying
I will multiply your descendant as the
stars of the heavens and as the sand*

*which is on the sea shore: and your
descendants shall possess the gates of
their enemies."*

[Genesis 22:17]

From the wilderness, the children of Israel
received all they needed to live on when
they reached Canaan. The wilderness
experience led to the promotion for
the children of Israel. The wilderness
experience of the children of Israel brought
victory, freedom and blessings to them.

Lessons

1. The wilderness experience may come
   with poverty and living from hand to
   mouth but our God is full of blessing.
   He made promises to Abraham and
   He never let him down. Therefore, if
   you are experiencing poverty, note
   that God knows and understands what
   He is doing:

2. If it was possible for the children
   of the Israel to be blessed in the
   wilderness which was supposed to
   be a place of dryness and waste,
   then it would be possible in your
   own situation too. Take heart from
   the fact that - *"Jesus Christ is the
   same yesterday, today and forever."*
   [Hebrews 13:8] No matter what you

have experienced in your darkest hour, whether bankruptcy, debt, financial instability, homelessness, joblessness, desertion by a loved one or bereavement, trust and commit your life totally to the Lord Jesus and He will surprise you. He reminds us:

"... do not worry about your life, what you will eat or what you will drink; nor about your body, what you will put on. Is life not more than food and the body more than cloth? Look at the birds of the air, for they neither sow nor reap... yet your heavenly father feeds them. Are you not of more value than they?"

[Matthew 6:25-26]

3. As God destroyed the hindrances to the blessings of the children of Israel, He is ready to destroy every obstacle to your progress both spiritually and materially, just believe in Him. The Bible warns us that - *"... our God is a consuming fire."* [Hebrews 12:29]

4. Though the vengeance of God came upon the Midianites and through this He blessed His people; yet the children of Israel were punished at Acacia Grove when they worshipped

Baal of Peor. Therefore, if you have at any time - now or in the past - sinned against God, your wilderness experience may be as a result of this sin. You must try to endure to the end as blessings are on your way:

"If you endure chastening, God deals with you as with sons; for what son is there whom a father does not chasten? But if you are without chastening, of which all have become partakers then you are illegitimate and not sons. Furthermore, you have had human fathers who corrected us, and we paid them respect. Shall we not much more readily be in subjection to the father of spirit and live?"
[Hebrews 12:7-9]

Whether or not we choose to obey God will determine our blessings:

"Now it shall come to pass, if you diligently obey the voice of the Lord your God, to observe carefully all His commandment ... Blessed shall you be in the city, and blessed shall you be in the country."
[Deuteronomy 28:1-3]

According to God's word, He blessed

the children of the Israel in the wilderness even though they did not totally obey his commandments. But because of Abraham's blessings, his descendants received the favour of God.

5. Satan also put Job through the wilderness of poverty but with God's consent. The Bible records that -

> *"So Satan answered the Lord and said, 'Does Job fear God for nothing? Have You not made a hedge around him, around his household, and around all that he has on every side? You have blessed the work of his hands, and his possessions have increased in the land. But now, stretch out Your hand and touch all that he has, and he will surely curse You to Your face!' and the Lord said to Satan, 'Behold, all that he has is in your power; only do not lay a hand on his person.'"*
>
> *[Job 1:9-12]*

Truly Satan caused Job to lose all he had in his life - children and livestock to the extent that his wife advised him to deny God. Yet he did not give away his integrity:

*"Far be it from me that I should
say you are right; till I die I will not
put away my integrity from me.
My righteousness I hold fast, and I
will not let it go; my heart shall not
reproach me as long as I live."*

[Job 27:5-6]

Job did not deny God but trusted Him
without question as He who gives and
takes away. At the end of the test,
Satan was defeated and departed with
shame but God blessed Job twice as
much as he had before his trials:

*"Now the Lord blessed the
latter days of Job more than the
beginning; for he had fourteen
thousand sheep, six thousand
camels... after this Job lived one
hundred and forty years, and saw
his children and grandchildren for
four generations."*

[Job 42:12-16]

God is also ready to bless you after
your wilderness test as long as you
are faithful to Him until the end.

6. The key to your success is praising,
    praying, fasting and meditating in
    the Word of God day and night. [1
    Thessalonians 5:16-18, Mark 9:29]

Chapter 10

Jesus Christ in the Wilderness

The New Testament, describes our Lord Jesus Christ as the *"author and finisher of our faith."* [Hebrews 12:2] He also passed through his own wilderness experience. Following His baptism, by John the Baptist, in the River Jordan:

> *"Jesus was led by the Spirit into the wilderness to be tempted by the devil"*
> *[Matthew 4:1]*

His own wilderness remains the perfect example of God's intention concerning the wilderness. In the wilderness, He fasted for forty days and forty nights and afterwards He was hungry. This was when Satan tempted Him because he knew that after the fasting He would naturally be hungry.

The wilderness acts a place of testing and sometimes becomes a battle ground for individuals, so too for Jesus, being tested by Satan to reveal whether He was ready, willing, and committed to save the whole world according His purpose on earth. Had Jesus failed the test, then it would have been Satan ruling the earth and we wouldn't have known the joy of salvation, but praise God Jesus never fails.

Jesus responded to all of Satan's temptations with the authority of God's Word. Don't forget that the Word of God is the sword of the Spirit [Ephesians 6:17] and that:

> *"The Word of God is living and powerful, and sharper than any two-edged sword, piercing even to the division of soul and spirit and of joint and marrow, and is a discerner of the thought and intents of the heart."*
>
> *[Hebrews 4:12]*

Satan tested Jesus in three main areas and we can expect to face the same kinds of temptations and tests in our own lives. Bear in mind that it is not a sin to be tempted but it is a sin to fail the test, and success will lead to spiritual and even material elevation.

Turn stones to bread

> *"And the devil said to Him, 'If You are the Son of God, command this stone to become bread' but Jesus answered him, saying, 'It is written, Man shall not live by bread alone, but by every*

word of God.'"

Jesus was hungry after forty days of fasting as any human being would naturally be; therefore Satan used the opportunity to test Him. He was tempted to use the power of his anointing to meet His own needs. [Matthew 27:40] Because Jesus had a sense of purpose - *"to serve, and to give His life a ransom for many"* [Mark 10:45], He responded with the Word of God. He declared - *"Man shall not live by bread alone, but by every word of God"* [Luke 4:4] This was also declared to the children of Israel in the wilderness. [Deuteronomy 8:3]

Lessons

1. Bread is not stone and can never become so except by supernatural intervention. Christ's wilderness experience remains a viable and most superb learning platform for all believers. Satan tempts Him to use His supernatural power to satisfy His human need. In the same way, Satan will seek to tempt us to fulfil for ourselves a need especially when we are under pressure - therefore, watch out and wait on God!

2. Obedience to God is more important

than personal gratification, comfort or success. Jesus was ordained to a purpose and was not going to be deflected from this. This a great lesson for you; no matter what it takes to get to your 'Canaan', do not turn your back but be an obedient servant.

3. If you like food or material comforts too much, you could easily fall into the trap of Satan. Instead, continue to feed yourself with the food from above. Jesus declared:

> *"I am the bread of life. He who comes to Me shall never hunger and he who believes in Me shall never thirsty."*
>
> *[John 6:35]*

Worship demanded in the wilderness

> *"Then the devil, taking Him up on a high mountain, showed Him all the kingdoms of the world in a moment of time, and the devil said to Him, 'All this authority I will give You, and their glory; for this has been delivered to me, and I give it to whomever I wish. Therefore, if You will worship before me, all will be Yours,' and Jesus answered and said to him, 'Get behind*

Me, Satan! for it is written, You shall worship the Lord your God, and Him only you shall serve.'"

[Luke 4:5-8]

Satan tempted Jesus to open a channel of a short-cut to gain. His goal was to put quick achievement before the principle of hard work and waiting on God. He was tempted to take an easier route to a desired end and to give up His divine purpose for an earthly reward. But thank God for Jesus Christ who preferred to suffer to achieve His purpose than going through a short route. He responded with the Word of God:

"You shall worship the Lord your God, and Him only you shall serve"

[Luke 4:8]

On a daily basis, Satan is demanding that every person bow down and worship him for a perishable reward rather than waiting to enjoy imperishable benefits. At every point of a believer's challenges, there will always be an alternative short cut that tends to undermine the purpose of God for man. God purposely formed man so that he can worship only Him, but Satan is seeking worship for himself.

The question is who do you bow to at the crossroad of challenges when you need to make a decision? Is it to gain the whole earth and lose heaven or to worship the Lord your God?

"Do you not know that to whom you present yourselves slaves to obey, you are that one's slaves whom you obey, whether of sin leading to death, or of obedience leading to righteousness?"

[Romans 6:16]

Think about this and make necessary corrections.

Lessons

1. Learn to do God's will His way and don't compromise. Do not allow your heart's desire or human influences to push you to sin against God.

   Remember that if you offend man you can be forgiven, but no mortal man can save you from the anger of God if you offend Him so watch out:

   "If one man sins against another, God will judge him. But if a man sins against the LORD, who will intercede for him?"

   [1 Samuel 2:25]

2. There is danger in getting our eyes fixed on someone or something

other than Jesus. It is important to discipline your eye as a believer since what you see can defile you. The Psalmist said:

"Turn away my eyes from looking at worthless things, and revive me in Your way"

[Psalms 119:37]

Worshipping a leader, doctrine, church or a ministry could lead to idolatry. Worship Jesus Christ only and not other gods.

Prove Yourself

"Then he brought Him to Jerusalem, set Him on the pinnacle of the temple, and said to Him, 'If You are the Son of God, throw Yourself down from here, for it is written: He shall give His angels charge over you, to keep you, and in their hands they shall bear you up, lest you dash your foot against a stone,' and Jesus answered and said to him, 'It has been said, you shall not tempt the Lord your God.'"

[Luke 4:9-12]

Jesus' very deity was being questioned by Satan, who tested His power and authority - *"... He shall give His angels charge over you ...*" Jesus responded with the Word of God.

Jesus responded with the same message of warning that God gave the children of Israel after they left Egypt:

"You shall not go after other gods, the gods of the peoples who are all around you (for the LORD your God is a jealous God among you), lest the anger of the LORD your God be aroused against you and destroy you from the face of the earth. You shall not tempt the LORD your God as you tempted Him in Massah."
[Deuteronomy 6:14-16]

Lessons

1. Satan can use the Word of God out of context as he used Psalms 91 - " *... for He shall give His angels charge over you ...*" [Psalm 91:11-12, Luke 4:10-11]

   He will try to do the same to confuse and deceive those who are not firmly rooted in faith just as he did to Christ. It is important that you know the Bible because Satan is very clever in confusing whoever is not well-rooted in the Word.

2. It is necessary that you know yourself to be a Child of God because Satan will also question your identity and faith and belief in Christ.

3. Watch out, don't let Satan use deceiving spirits to get you out of the Book of Life and Kingdom of God through his cunning questions and doctrinal issues. Don't forget that through sweet words he deceived Eve in the garden of Eden and when Adam sinned, they lost the glory of God. [1 Timothy 2:4, 2 Corinthians 11:3 & Romans 5:12]

Even though Jesus was alone and seemed forgotten in the wilderness during the temptation by Satan yet God was with Him:

"And He was there in the wilderness forty days tempted by Satan, and was with the wild beasts; and the angels ministered to Him"

[Mark 1:13]

It may seem that you are alone and forgotten in your problems, but don't panic - just trust that God is with you. Even after victory over the problems, never let down your guard knowing that the earth is a spiritual battle front:

*"Now when the devil had ended
every temptation, he departed from
Him until an opportune time."*

[Luke 4:13]

If the devil could depart for an
opportune time concerning Jesus
Christ, then don't abandon your
spiritual armour because Satan is
never at rest:

*"Be sober, be vigilant; because
your adversary the devil walks
about like a roaring lion seeking
whom he may devour."*

[1 Peter 5:8]

Steps to victory during temptations

Prayer is the first key to the breakthrough
during temptation. Jesus actually said to
the disciples that we should pray so that
we are not give in to temptation - *"Watch
and pray, lest you enter into temptation ..."*
[Matthew 26:41] However, if we find ourselves
in the trap of temptation, we need to seek
the face of God for victory.

The scripture says:

*"Resist the devil and he will flee from
you."* [James 4:7]

"Flee also youthful lust; but pursue righteousness..." [2 Timothy 2:22]

"Flee sexual immorality..." [1 Corinthians 6:18]

"Therefore, my beloved, flee from idolatry." [1 Corinthians 10:14]

"For the love of money is a root of all kinds of evil ..." [1 Timothy 6:11]

Use the Word of God because what was written in the Old Testament was the weapon that gave Jesus the victory during His temptations:

"But He answered and said, 'It is written, man shall not live by bread alone, but by every word that proceeds from the mouth of God.'" [Matthew 4:4]

"So He humbled you, allowed you to hunger, and fed you with manna which you did not know nor did your fathers know, that He might make you know that man shall not live by bread alone; but man lives by every word that proceeds from the mouth of the LORD" [Deuteronomy 8:3]

"Jesus said to him, 'It is written again, you shall not tempt the LORD your God.'" [Matthew 4:7]

"You shall not tempt the LORD your God as you tempted Him in Massah"
[Deuteronomy 6:16]

Search the Scriptures to know the Word so that faith can spring forth in order to stand firm in the evil day.

Chapter 11

The World as the Darkest Wilderness

This world is the darkest wilderness. Jesus has gone to prepare a place elsewhere for us and promises to return for us. [John 14:1-6] Where He has gone there is everlasting light and joy.

He further explained the realisation of the absolute vanity of this present world to us in the parable of the sower where He explained that:

> *"The field is the world, the good seeds are the sons of the kingdom, but the tares are the sons of the wicked one"*
> *[Matthew 13:38]*

This world is an only route to the Eternal Kingdom. It is essential for every believer to pass through this present evil world, as a wilderness, to discern those things which are abhorrent to God. Jesus was tested in three ways just as all Christians are.

The wilderness is a place of waste and arid dryness. Before anything good can come out of a wilderness, the farmer has to work hard to irrigate the land. The plan of the farmer is to turn the wilderness into fruitful land - this represents the plan of God. For every believer, the world is the wilderness where we face hardship, problems and battles before we can reach our Canaan. It was the Spirit of God who led Jesus into the wilderness to be tempted; and so too the Holy Spirit may at times direct us to meet Satan for our spiritual development. Jesus warned us that:

> *"If they persecuted Me, they will also persecute you; if they kept My word they will keep yours also. But all these things they will do to you for My name's sake..."*
>
> *[John 15:20]*

Persecution will arise because you are a Child of God; they will hate you because of Jesus. Yet, you must take up your cross and follow without looking back, having in mind that our everlasting home is with Christ in His Father's house. Knowing that we have a short period to spend here because we are just passing through, we must try as much as possible to *"make our calling and election sure."* [2 Peter 1:10]

Though the world is the wilderness, the greatest battle is within ourselves in the battlefield of the heart. Friends and family may desert you, enemies may attack and financial pressure may intensify; but if we don't sin against God, all these will only lead to promotion but sin against God will lead to destruction in hell's fire.

Lessons

1. Each time Satan is at work in your heart, learn to use the Word of God, the sword of the Spirit, to fight as it is the greatest weapon. God's Word always brings deliverance:

   "Then they cried out to the Lord in their trouble, And He saved them out of their distresses. He sent His word and healed them, and delivered them from their destructions."
   [Psalms 107:19-20]

2. Do not rest in the wilderness [do not give up] as Satan does not rest. If Jesus passed through the wilderness of this world and Satan tempted him, you will also face temptations, but we are exhorted to flee from temptation and resist the devil steadfastly. The crown of life awaits those who refuse to let temptation get the better of them:

"Blessed is man who endures temptation; for when he has been approved, he will receive the crown of life which the Lord has promised to those who love Him."

[James 1:12]

Chapter 12

The Promised Canaan

The scripture confirmed that the promise of God for the children of Israel came to pass as He said:

> *"Not a word failed of any good thing which the Lord had spoken to the house of Israel, all came to pass."*
> *[Joshua 21:45]*

They arrived at a land flowing with milk and honey as a nation but not every individual who set out on the journey made it. Though they had been rescued physically from Egypt, many maintained the slave mentality and in desiring their past life, they had rebelled against God.

The battle on the outside is always easier to conquer than the battle on the inside. An adage restates this – *"if the enemy within does not kill then the external enemy cannot."* The heart of man is the spiritual wilderness and battlefield where we wrestle every day and Canaan is our heavenly home. We are told that:

> *"The Son of Man will send out His angels, and they will gather out of His*

*kingdom all things that offend, and
those who practice lawlessness, and
will cast them into the furnace of fire.
There will be wailing and gnashing of
teeth. Then the righteous will shine
forth as the sun in the kingdom of their
Father. He who has ears to hear, let
him hear!"*

Matthew 13:41-43

Consider the following points

1. Continuous renewal of the mind is essential so that the devil will not defeat us:

   "And be not conformed to this world, but be transformed by the renewing of your mind, that you may prove what is that good and acceptable and perfect will of God."

   [Romans 12:2]

2. *"Put on the whole armour of God, that you may be able to stand against the wiles of the devil"* [Ephesians 6:11] Do this at all times for we do not wrestle against flesh and blood but against principalities, powers, rulers of the darkness of this age and spiritual hosts of wickedness in the heavenly places.

The Armour of God consists of the Belt of Truth, the Breastplate of Righteousness, Feet shod with the preparation of the Gospel of Peace, the Shield of Faith, the Helmet of Salvation, and the sword of the Spirit which is the Word of God.

3. Just as Canaan flowed with milk and honey, heaven is full of joy. Whoever serves Jesus Christ in truth and in spirit without looking back will inherit all things. God promises that :

"He who overcomes shall inherit all things, and I will be his God and he shall be My son"

[Revelation 21:7]

4. The scripture confirmed that the children of Israel eventually had peace from all the surrounding nations:

"The Lord gave them rest all around, according to all that He had sworn to their fathers. And not a man of all their enemies stood against them. The Lord delivered all their enemies into their hand."

[Joshua 21:44]

So also God will give rest to whoever overcomes eventually all old things must pass away before God will accept anyone to heaven:

> " *Then Peter said, 'See, we have left all and followed You.' So He said to them, 'Assuredly, I say to you, there is no one who has left house or parents or brothers or wife or children, for the sake of the Kingdom of God, who shall not receive many times more in this present time, and in the age to come eternal life.'*"
>
> *[Luke 18:28-30]*

5. The land of Canaan inherited by the children of Israel is described as good and large land flowing with milk and honey. Though eternal benefits cannot be equated with earthly Canaan enjoyment, in this context, our spiritual Canaan - heaven, is described in the Bible as follows -

> "*... the great city, the holy Jerusalem descending out of heaven from God having the glory of God. Her light was like a most precious stone, like a jasper stone, clear as crystal.*"
>
> *[Revelation 21:10-11]*

The Apostle John goes on to

describe the construction of the wall, the street and the light including the water in the city -

"The construction of its wall was of jasper; and the city was pure gold, like clear glass. The foundations of the wall of the city were adorned with all kinds of precious stones... The city had no need of the sun or of the moon to shine in it, for the glory of God illuminated it. The lamb is its light... a pure river of water of life, clear as crystal proceeding from the throne of God and the Lamb."

[Revelation 21:10-23]

This is what is waiting for everyone who walks in the wilderness of this world and overcomes. God is looking for people like Joshua who will follow Him fully without looking left or right and without going back to spiritual slavery. Such are the people of whom Jesus Christ said:

"If anyone loves Me, he will keep My word; and My Father will love him, and We will come to him and make Our home with him."

[John 14:23]

In addition to this, Jesus said such people will live with Him in His Fathers' house:

> "*Blessed and holy is he who has part in the first resurrection. Over such the second death has no power, but they shall be priests of God and of Christ, and shall reign with Him a thousand years*"
>
> *[Revelation 20:6]*

This opportunity of reigning with Jesus is still open for you now; therefore, if you are still living in sin, ask for forgiveness today and forsake your sin so that you can also inherit your eternal Canaan:

> "*For whoever desire to save his life will lose it, but whoever loses his life for My sake will find it. For what profit is it to a man if he gains the whole world, and loses his own soul, or what will a man give in exchange for his soul?*"
>
> *[Matthew 16:25-26]*

The Apostle Paul advised us - "*...Work out your salvation with fear and trembling.*" *[Philippians 2:12]* in order to qualify to be with God for eternity.

Chapter 13

No Canaan Without Deliverance from the Powers of Darkness

The strongholds of ancient Egypt included slavery, poverty, witchcraft, wizardry, marine powers:

> *"You are wearied in the multitude of your counsels; Let now the astrologers, the stargazers, and the monthly prognosticators stand up and save you from what shall come upon you."*
>
> *[Isaiah 47:13]*

Without proper deliverance from the Land of Egypt, you cannot reach Canaan. The children of Israel were taken out of the land of slavery with the intention of settling them in the land of freedom. They were delivered from their past in order to live peacefully in their present life but they refused to accept the offer God gave them. They preferred the land of slavery to the land of freedom. The evidences of these were established in the way they complained on their way in the wilderness:

> *"... in their hearts they turned back to*

*Egypt, saying to Aaron, 'Make us gods
to go before us...'"*

[Acts 7:39-40]

and

*"... let us alone that we may serve
the Egyptians? For it would have been
better for us to serve the Egyptians
than that we should die in the
wilderness."*

[Exodus 14:12]

They even got to a point that they blamed
God for their predicament and decided to
return to Egypt. They preferred to go back
to slavery when God promised greater
things for them:

*"Why has the Lord brought us to this
land to fall by the sword, that our
wives and children should become
victims? Would it not be better for us
to return to Egypt? So they said to
one another let us select a leader and
return to Egypt."*

[Numbers 14:3-4]

Through these statements we can see that
the children of Israel were truly delivered
from the physical but not the spiritual
slavery of their minds.

A perfect and total deliverance always

includes the physical and spiritual - that is deliverance from external and internal bondage. Since defilement comes from within, cleansing or deliverance should also come from within:

> *"But those things which proceed out of the mouth come from the heart, and they defile a man. For out of the heart proceed evil thoughts, murders, adulteries, fornication, thefts, false witness, blasphemies."*
> *[Matthew 15:18-19]*

When the mind is free from the bondage of sin, then the body will automatically accept the deliverance and act on the freedom given. [1 Thessalonians 5:23]

Jesus has delivered each human generation from the slavery of sin that our forefathers brought about in the garden of Eden:

> *"For since by man came death, by Man also came the resurrection of the dead. For as in Adam all die, even so in Christ all shall be made alive"*
> *[1 Corinthians 15:21-22]*

Truly Jesus reconciled us all back to God by shedding His own blood for the atonement of our sins. Each individual must decide whether or not to accept this free gift.

Have you truly repented? God loved the children of Israel so much that He sent Moses to deliver them from slavery but they sabotaged their own freedom. God declared:

> "But this is what I commanded them, saying, 'obey My voice, and I will be your God, and you shall be My people. And walk in all the ways that I have commanded you, that it may be well with you.' Yet they did not obey or incline their ear, but followed the counsels and dictates of their evil hearts, and went backward and not forward."
>
> [Jeremiah 7:23-24]

Jesus has delivered you, so why not move forward by living in the joy of salvation instead of looking back to the past?

Remember Lot's wife looked back and became a pillar of salt; the children of Israel looked back and they died in the wilderness. We have the opportunity to learn from this so that we will not make the same mistake:

> "For whatever things were written before were written for our learning, that we through the patience and comfort of the Scriptures might have

hope"
[Roman 15:4]

And if your deliverance is only on your tongue, in other words you are confessing Jesus as your Lord and Saviour but still living in sin, you may need proper deliverance. It may be that you have only experienced half-deliverance like the children of Israel in which case you must complete it in order to enjoy Jesus fully and to reign with Him at His second coming. The Apostle Paul warns us that:

> *"... flesh and blood cannot inherit the kingdom of God; nor does corruption inherit incorruption."*
>
> *[1 Corinthians 15:50]*

Steps to perfect and complete deliverance

Be born again and present your bodies as living sacrifices holy and acceptable to God and do not be conformed to this world. [Romans 12:1-2] Make every effort to live holy for God is Holy.

Consider the source of Israel's troubles. Similarly, what happened in your past that is affecting your present success? Have you ever joined the occult, witchcraft or any evil society? You need to recognise it and repent.

Reject the unprofitable tenants whom the scriptures refer to as strangers. [Psalms 18:43-45] Reject the evils of your heart, confess the evil you have done now or in the past to Jesus and promise not to go back to your sins anymore. Remove the fetish doctor's materials and or 'fudu'[1] hidden in every corner of your house and more importantly the ones in your body and soul:

"Thus says the Lord GOD: 'Woe to the women who sew magic charms on their sleeves and make veils for the heads of people of every height to hunt souls! Will you hunt the souls of My people, and keep yourselves alive?...' Therefore thus says the Lord GOD: 'Behold, I am against your magic charms by which you hunt souls there like birds. I will tear them from your arms, and let the souls go, the souls you hunt like birds.'"

[Ezekiel 13:18-20]

Repair what was damaged when you were still under bondage to Egypt. [Egypt

---

1 Fudu - also known as voodoo or charm produced by a 'fetish doctor' to 'make' or 'mess up' peoples' lives. The unhealthy use of such materials can also cause disasters in marriage, home, work and other areas. Extract from 'Woman Warfare Weapon' by Rev Stella Adekunle 2014; Jesus Joy Publishing page 21.

represents slavery to sin] Prayer and fasting will help in repairing what Satan has damaged through the sin of the past. Jesus described certain demonic strongholds:

> *"However, this kind does not go out except by prayer and fasting."*
> [Matthew 17:21]

Persist in seeking the guidance of the Holy Spirit. Just as the believers in the Bible were consistently filled by the Spirit and by the gift of wisdom, you also need to be filled constantly in order to have a successful journey in this world. [2 Peter 1:3-10]

Chapter 14

Key Milestones of the Wilderness Journey

These are the milestones on the journey of the children of Israel who went out of the land of Egypt by their armies under the hand of Moses and Aaron.

They departed from Rameses on the day after Passover. The children of Israel went out with boldness in the sight of King Pharaoh and all the Egyptians for they were burying all their first born whom the Lord had killed among them.

The children of Israel moved from Ramose and camped at Succoth, they departed from there and camped at Etham which is on the edge of the wilderness. They moved from there and turned back to Pi Hahirpth which is the east of Baal Zephon; and they camped near Migdon. They departed from before Hahiroth and passed through the midst of the sea (Red Sea) into the wilderness, when three days journey in the wilderness of Etham, and camped at Marah. [bitter water turned to sweet]

They moved from there and turned to
Elim where twelve springs of water and
seventy palm trees are so they camped
there. They moved from Elim and
camped by the Red sea. They moved
from the Red sea and camped at the
wilderness of sin. [where God fed them
with bread from heaven]

They journeyed in the Wilderness of
Sin and camped at Dophkah, they
departed from there and camped at
Alush. They moved from Alush and
camped at Rephidim where there
was no water for the people to drink
and God supplied water through the
instruction from God that Moses should
strike the rod by the rod of God in his
hand at Horeb.

They departed from Rephidim
and camped in the wilderness
of Sinai where God gave the ten
commandments. They moved
from there and camped at Kibroth
Hattaavah, they departed from
there and camped at Hazeroth. They
departed from Hazeroth and camped at
Rithmah and from there they camped
at Rimmon Perez and from there to
Libnah. They moved from Libnah and

camped at Rissah.

They journeyed from there and
camped at Kehelathah. They went
from there and camped at mount
Shepherd. They moved from there
and camped at Haradah and moved
to camp at Makheloth and camped
at Tahath. They moved from there
and camped at Terah, from Terah to
Mithkah. They moved from Mithkah to
Hashmonah, they departed from there
to Moseroth from there to Ben Jaakan.
They moved from there and camped
at Hor Hagidgad. They moved from
there and camped at Jotbathah. They
moved from Jotbathah and camped at
Abronah. They departed from there to
Ezion Geber from there to wilderness
of Zin which is Kadesh. They moved
from there to mount Hor on the
boundary of the land of Edom, Haron
(Aaron) the priest died on mount Hor
according to the commandment of the
Lord and he was hundred and twenty
three years when he died.

The children of Israel departed from
mount Hor and camped at Zalmonah,
then departed from there and camped
at Punon.

They departed from there and camped

at Oboth, they departed from there and camped at Ije Abarim at the border of Moab, they departed from Ije Abarin and camped at Dibion-Gad. They moved from there and camped at Almon-Diblathaim they moved from there and camped in the mountains Abarim before Nebo. They departed from the mountains of Abarim and camped in the plains of Moab by the Jordan, across from Jericho, they camped by the Jordan from Beth Jesimoth as far as the Abel Acacia Groove in the plains of Moab where God spoke to Moses concerning Cannan:

"Speak to the children of Israel and say to them: when you have crossed the Jordan into the land of Canaan, then you shall drive out all the inhabitant of the land form before you, destroy all there engraved stones, destroy all the moulded images, and demolish all their high places;' You shall disposes the inhabitants of the land and dwell in it for I have given you the land to possess"
[Numbers 33:51-53]

Ten Keys For a Successful Christian

Journey In The Wilderness

1. Know your God

"And even as they did not like to retain God in their knowledge, God gave them over to a debased mind, to do those things which are not fitting"

[Romans 1:28]

Those who do not know their God will end up sinning during the time of challenges. With sadness of mind, I recalled visiting a foreign country to minister where I met some ladies who were immigrants and felt they had no choice but to sell their bodies for money since they couldn't communicate in the local language. I believe that there were some who said *"No"* to such temptation. This an example of a wildness journey where a serious decision has to be made. Those who trust their God will do great exploit. As God didn't leave the Israelite in their wilderness, He will definitely come through for whoever can stand firm in faith.

2. Listen to instruction

As a Christian in the wilderness journey of life with the understanding that the wilderness comes in the shape of problems and challenges of life, it is imperative to look up to the author and the finisher of our faith - Jesus Christ. The wilderness journey of Abraham required that he patiently wait for the promised seed, Isaac, but he ended up bringing forth Ishmael. Any inpatient brother or sister in the wilderness who is seeking the face of God for the fruit of the womb may end up birthing Ishmael instead of Isaac.

3. Focus on the Captain of the Army

No matter the noise of the people around you in the wilderness , you must remain focused. Job could easily have lost patience with the 'unfriendly' friends who were his comforters during his challenges. His wife even told him to deny his God. The journey of life can be rough, tough and full of turbulence but always check that you are still in Christ. The wife of Lot looked back and became a pillar of salt:

> "Examine yourselves as to whether you are in the faith. Test yourselves. Do you not know yourselves, that Jesus Christ is in you? - unless indeed you are disqualified"
>
> [2 Corinthians 13:5]

4. Do not fear

Not only will fear not change our circumstances, but were assured that - *"God has not given us a spirit of fear, but of power and of love and of a sound mind."* [2 Timothy 1:7] David was able to face Goliath with boldness. He carefully chose his words to antagonise Goliath' threat. It is only the fearless that can win the fearful battles in the wilderness of life. Goliath had seen people running away from him but he lost it when he saw a small boy running to attack him. Whatever your challenge, learn to face it with boldness and not fear.

5. Do not be dismayed

Worries only help to expand the problem. Jesus reasoned with his disciples in order to convince them that stress and anxiety were to no avail:

> *"And which of you by worrying can add one cubit to his stature? If you then are not able to do the least, why are you anxious for the rest?"*
>
> *[Luke 12:25-26]*

6. Know your weapon and how to use effectively

The effective weapon in the wilderness of the Israelite journey was the rod of

Moses and sometimes Aaron. The most effective weapons in our wilderness experiences are the word of God, blood of Jesus Christ and praying in the spirit.

7. Know the Word of God

What has already been written is for own benefits:

> *"For whatever things were written before were written for our learning, that we through the patience and comfort of the Scriptures might have hope."*
>
> [Romans 15:4]

8. Have a violent faith

Christians without a violent faith cannot move mountains:

> *"But someone will say, 'You have faith, and I have works. Show me your faith without your works, and I will show you my faith by my works.'"*
>
> [James 2:18]

> *"Since the time of John the Baptist the kingdom of God suffers violent and the violent take it by force."*
>
> [Matthew 11:12]

Satan is not willing to release anything in his possession without a fight.

Therefore, you need all the faith at your disposal to pull through the problems of life. May God help us all.

9. Believe in His prophets

"... Jehoshaphat stood and said, 'Hear me, O Judah and you inhabitants of Jerusalem: Believe in the LORD your God, and you shall be established; believe His prophets, and you shall prosper.'"

[2 Chronicles 20:20]

There are still genuine servants of God who are truly called and who are doing the work of God fearfully and faithfully. Listen to them and take instructions that will help you on your journey. Moses and Aaron led the people of God through the wilderness and successfully handed the mantle of leadership over to Joshua. I pray that God will connect you to your own Moses and Aaron in Jesus' name.

10. Strategically plan your journey

The way of the individual in the wilderness of problems differs from one person to another. Therefore it is not profitable to compare your wilderness experience with other people around you. The Bible says:

"For we dare not class ourselves or

*compare ourselves with those who
commend themselves. But they,
measuring themselves by themselves,
and comparing themselves among
themselves, are not wise"*
[2 Corinthians 10:12]

It took only a stone to bring Goliath to his
knees but in the case of Joshua, all he had
to say was - *"Sun, stand still over Gibeon;
And Moon, in the Valley of Aijalon"* [Joshua
10:12] before Adoni-Zedek was brought to
his knees. Whenever there are challenges,
the Holy Spirit and the Scriptures are
the perfect road map to guide you to a
successful end. It is not wise for man to
do it in his own way, for - *"there is a way
that seems right to a man but the end is
destruction."* [Proverbs 16:25] Nor should you
seek for alternatives:

*"And when they say to you, 'Seek
those who are mediums and wizards,
who whisper and mutter,' should not
a people seek their God? Should they
seek the dead on behalf of the living?"*
[Isaiah 8:19]

Remember king Saul sought out a medium
and came back with a death sentence. It is
important at this point to call your attention
to the fact that the road to the city of God
 - The New Jerusalem which comes out

of heaven - is not an easy one. For it is
written:

> "Narrow is the gate and difficult is the
> way which leads to life, and there are
> few who find it"
>
> *[Matthew 7:14]*

Learn to trust absolutely in God, through
the Holy Spirit's direction and with the
understanding of what the Word of God
says about the matter. Then you will
successfully win your battles. Confess
boldly that - *"Your word is a lamp to my
feet And a light to my path."* [Psalms 119:105]
Surely, He will not disgrace nor put you to
shame.

Chapter 15

The Spiritual Giants in the Wilderness of Life

The wilderness is a giant that all believers must practically experience. There is no way we can journey through this Christian life without a wilderness. Israel as a nation reached the earthly promised land as this was the promise God had made to their forefathers. God struck down many individuals in the wilderness and many lost their lives because of sins committed along the way.

Where you are concerned, God's promise stands for your life no matter what you have gone through or what you are going through now. You simply need to believe in the power that can change the unchangeable, and as the Apostle Paul recommends "... *work out your own salvation with fear and trembling.*" [Philippians 2:12]

The Wilderness is literally a school of 'hard knocks' where strengths are measured in accordance with the various situations experienced along the way. Our wilderness experiences as believers can include loneliness, prayer, fasting, hunger and the only company seems to be Satan just as Jesus Christ experienced all these in His wilderness experience. Let me also call your attention to the fact that Canaan represents a divine location for you as a person in your relationship with God. It is important to note that the children of Israel only entered Canaan but never enjoyed the 'milk and honey of the land' because there was a condition attached to it which they did not fulfil. To enter the land is unconditional but to enjoy its milk and honey is conditional. This means that even if you endure the wilderness, permanent rest is not guaranteed unless you fulfil the conditions. The following passage makes this clear:

"Then the Angel of the Lord came up from Gilgal to Bochim, and said: 'I led you up from Egypt and brought you to the land of which I swore to your fathers; and I said, I will never break My covenant with you, and you shall make no covenant with the inhabitants of this land; you shall tear down their altars. But you have not obeyed My voice. Why have you done this? Therefore I also said, I will not drive them out before you; but they shall be thorns in your side, and their gods

shall be a snare to you.'"

[Judges 2:1-3]

As the size of your vision is, so also will be the dimension of your wilderness. As big as your farmland, so also your labour will be. It is a testing period. Hunger or desire still remains the perfect method of testing for the human race and creation as seen in the case of Adam and Eve in the Old Testament and our Lord Jesus Christ in the New Testament.

Hunger has two definitions - desire for food and also any strong desire. Note that when any strong desire comes, there will be a forbidden 'food' around. For example:

- David's son Amon's lust for Tamar.

- Abraham travelling to Egypt for the sake of acquiring food to eat.

- Jacob who kept all his family in a strange land [Egypt] because of food.

- Esau who sold his birthright because of food.

This hunger is represented by the 'stone' that Satan tempted Jesus to turn to bread. This Satanic arrangement is sometimes permitted by God for the purpose of testing. We are all students and we must be

tested or examined before promotion.
He who is hungry for money may use
his child, wife, or steal and the like.

He who is hungry for sex may use just
anybody available even his own daughter,
that is 'stone' in a figurative sense. In the
wilderness of temptation, our Lord Jesus
Christ said to His disciples that His food is:

> *"to do the will of He who sent Him and
> to accomplish it."*
>
> *[John 4:31]*

Have you identified your own wilderness? Is
it poverty, financial hardship, persecution or
tribulation? Are you in debt or living from
hand to mouth? Remember that God is in
control, riches come from the Lord and at
the right time He will definitely bless you
if you trust him. If it is possible for Jesus
to feed five thousand with two fishes and
five loaves of bread and still have extra
food to spare [Mark 8:19], your wilderness
experience will similarly not be impossible
to overcome.

Conclusion

Whatever your wilderness experience, strive hard to get through it. Paul the Apostle said:

> *"Not that I have already attained, or am already perfected; but I press on, that I may lay hold of that for which Christ Jesus has also laid hold of me."*
> *[Philippians 3:12]*

Each day brings different experiences and people into our lives. Not all experiences will be pleasant or comfortable. In the journey of life, our 'Red Sea' may be like that of the Apostle Paul who recounted his various trials and tribulations:

> *"... in perils of waters, in perils of robbers, in perils of my own countrymen, in perils of the Gentiles, in perils in the city, in perils in the wilderness, in perils in the sea, in perils among false brethren."*
> *[2 Corinthians 11:26]*

No matter how dark it may look, please don't give up as there is always a way out of the tunnel. I have faced different challenges from co-workers, and fellow countrymen. I join with the Apostle Paul in declaring:

> *"Brethren, I do not count myself to have apprehended; but one thing I do, forgetting those things which are behind and reaching forward to those things which are ahead, I press toward the goal for the prize of the upward call of God in Christ Jesus."*
>
> *[Philippians 3:13-14]*

May God count us all worthy of His kingdom, in Jesus' name.

Prayer Points

- In my own land of slavery, O Lord, send me a Moses for my rescue as you did for the Israelites in the land of Egypt.

- Lord, always be a 'pillar of cloud' for me by day and a 'pillar of fire' at night through the wilderness of my life as you were for the Israelites in the wilderness.

- Make a way for me, O Lord, whenever it seems there is no way as you parted the Red Sea for the children of Israel.

- As the rod of God in Moses' hand turned to a snake and swallowed up the snakes of the Egyptian magicians, O Lord, let a divinely-appointed snake swallow the snakes of all the enemies in my life.

- As You used the east wind to pave the way for the children of Israel at the Red Sea and used the same wind to destroy Pharaoh and his chariots, O Lord, let Your east wind comfort me and let it destroy every Pharaoh in my life.

- Lord, plant your fear in my life so that I will never disobey You. Continuously fill me with the fire of the Holy Spirit.

- Bearing in mind that Satan used the children of Israel and pushed Moses against God, O Lord, do not allow Satan to use me against myself, anyone around me or against God.

- Lord, no matter what I am going through, do not let me look back to the land of slavery but give me the grace to continue to go forward. Also, help me not to bow down to other gods.

- Lord, send down the fire of the Holy Ghost to destroy every 'spirit of

Egypt' in my Life and set me free of all bondage.

- Lord, grant me the power to rely totally on the food and drink from heaven which is obtained through the Word of God and the power of prayer.

- Lord, break into pieces by your heavenly thunder every wall of Jericho built around me and lead me to my blessing.

- *"My God is a consuming fire."* [Hebrew 13:29] Therefore, O Lord, prove Yourself as consuming fire of every Satanic audience all around me and give me peace.

- Lord, bless me in the wilderness of this world as you have blessed the children of Israel in their wilderness journey.

- Lord, help me to get to the promised land of my life as You did for the children of Israel and don't let me die at the battlefront.

- Lord, send your heavenly warriors to fight the battle of my life.

- As You led the children of Israel

through the wilderness, O Lord, lead me throughout the days of my life and destroy every hindrance and stumbling block on my way with a heavenly earthquake.

- Lord, show me your divine mercy and favour all along the wilderness of my life just as you showed the children of Israel your divine favour in their wilderness journey.

- Lord, give me victory over the wilderness experience of my life, and just as You did not put the children of Israel to shame, don't let me be put to shame.

- Lord as You put Pharaoh and the Egyptian magicians to shame over the children of Israel, put every 'Luciferian troubler' of my life to shame and let them bow to your Name in my life.

- Lord, give me the strength to stand in the wilderness of my life and uphold me till I get to the promised land in heaven.

In Jesus' name I pray, Amen.

Also By The Author

Woman Warfare Weapon

ISBN 9781907971396

Looking at our world today, the hearts of many women are crying and asking for revenge. Many are wondering where it all went wrong and some allow bitterness, hatred and anger to fester in their minds because of the wounds they incurred from men during courtship or in marriage, and from fathers or father figures.

Some need deliverance from their darkened mind, sorrowful past and faulty foundation, caused by self-error, family background or deception from the chief priests of Satan.

Many women have been tied down and tormented under indescribable bondage and unbearable burdens like the Israelites in the land of Egypt. It's time for them to experience freedom and gain deliverance from witchcraft and the marine kingdom to enjoy the life that Jesus came to give in abundance [John 10:10].

Elijah: Prophet of Fire
ISBN 9789780808631

Elijah the prophet of fire is one of best selling books on the market that explains the powerful power of God in action in the life of prophet Elijah. It exposes an exemplary operation of the prophet of the scripture and guiding the reader into exercise their God giving authority over the power of darkness.

It presents fresh insight and facts that our Lord Jesus Christ is still at work just as the time of old. *"Jesus Christ is same yesterday, today and forever"*. Biblical exposition in the Elijah prophet of fire is most powerful Sunday school lectures material ever written.

Battle Cry Against Strongholds

This book is specially written to open the understanding of the children of God to the reality of the operation of the kingdom of darkness. The book is designed to lift up the ancient gates and everlasting doors that are operating at the edge of breakthroughs. It is aimed at opening the prison doors for

those in Satanic captivity so that they can walk free.

This book is targeted at releasing the possessions of the children of God held in the *"strong man's"* warehouse. Many destinies have been buried under the sea and rivers of life by the enemy without the knowledge of their owners of the destinies.

Crossing Your Jordan

ISBN 9789780808624

This book is an eye opener to every child of God about the activities of the enemy. It concentrates on issues relating to how the enemy operates invisibly and manifests itself visibly.

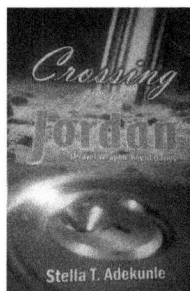

It is a concise, do-it-yourself collection of prayers, designed to be utilised in your own way for prompt deliverance and freedom from the enemy. Therefore, the book is a weapon of warfare and training artillery for every child of God seeking deliverance from the hands of the enemy. It is also useful for those who simply desire to enhance their Christian prayer life.

Various Evangelical Tracts

All available from SSEO at their website:

www.sseooutreach.org.uk

www.ingramcontent.com/pod-product-compliance
Lightning Source LLC
Chambersburg PA
CBHW070105070426
42448CB00038B/1669